"In **Step Up and Stand Out**,
masterfully shows introverts how to harness
their superpowers to succeed in the workplace
– their way. From how to speak up in meetings
and provide valuable solutions, to how to create
relationships infused with trust and
acknowledge your accomplishments in front of
supervisors and team members, **Step Up and
Stand Out** should be required reading for all
introverts."

Alexia Vernon, President and Author,
Step into Your Moxie

"The 20 tips outlined offer readers insight into
becoming that stand-out leader without
compromising who they are so that they can use
their passions to thrive in their careers and live
in their purpose. But it doesn't stop there. **Step
Up and Stand Out** offers insight to CEOs, top-
level executives, and extroverts, such as myself,
on how to recognize the talents of the introverts
on their team and how to coach introverted
leaders. Recognizing the talents of all types of
leaders not only promotes diversity in the
workplace, which increases creativity and
innovation, but provides a variety of different
and new perspectives, thus creating a more
inclusive workplace. As a leader who is always
looking for ways to grow and tools that will help
the leaders on my team, I highly recommend this
book."

Dr. Kiki Ramsey, Founder/CEO of
The Positive Psychology Coaching and
Diversity Institute

"There's so much goodness to take from this book, and Tip #15 (Own Your Story) is my favorite. The leaders who have the highest trust and retention on their teams own their stories...and they allow the people around them to do the same. Heather's book is full of important nuggets for all of us who identify as introverted leaders, and offers helpful ways to take the work deeper. This book is a leadership companion that helps you do the important internal work that will have ripple effects far out into the world."

Lara Heacock, MBA, PCC, Leadership & Executive Coach for leaders with the audacity to bring kindness into business.

"I take pride in endorsing Heather, both as a trusted leader whom I have had the pleasure of knowing, working with from a distance, and learning from over the past few years, and her new book **Stand Up and Stand Out**. As a recognized Leader of Leaders myself, who has led teams of 450+ and still leading teams today, and an author of over 30 ghostwritten leadership books, I believe I have earned the privilege to recognize a quality work that will benefit many. I encourage you to read her first work, and then engage with Heather; your life will be greatly strengthened and you will gain new and exciting perspectives to be challenged and grow."

Jeff Brewer, Senior Sales Manager, PerkinElmer Foods Division

"When I was working in a corporate setting, I know I often felt stressed and underappreciated, and yet I could never quite put my finger on why. The first aha was when I discovered I am an "outgoing" introvert. Reading Heather's book offered even more insight as to why I felt so out of my comfort zone in many situations, as I saw my past corporate self mirrored in the stories she tells and nodding along in agreement with the wisdom she shares. In **Step Up and Stand Out**, Heather shares thoughtful inspiration and tips on how introverts can embrace who they are, honor what they need, and grow into feeling confident and empowered. It's a powerful book in a tiny package and I highly recommend it."

> **Paula Jenkins**, Podcast Producer, Strategist, and host of *Jump Start Your Joy* and *Joy of Podcasting*

"Heather wrote this book for those who may see themselves as introverts, struggling to be heard in a loud, brash business world. However, I think the content is relevant regardless of personality. The insightful chapters and topics will resonate with those in leadership or aspiring to get there. The chapters are easy to digest and embrace. It will help you build confidence and make your endeavors more satisfying. Keep this book close – a handy reference before your next interview or important meeting. Making your voice heard will pay huge dividends personally, professionally, and for your organization."

> **Dave Smercina**, CEO and President of Smercina & Associates Advisory

"Corporate culture often means the loudest and the boldest become the voices most heard. Unfortunately, thriving in that culture can leave introverts feeling unseen, unappreciated, and often overlooked for leadership roles. Drawing from experience, Heather offers practical and heartfelt guidance for these aspiring leaders in her book, **Step Up and Stand Out**. Tips include physically taking a seat at the table, doing the inner work of self-acceptance, and even wearing something with pockets! We all love pockets, but who knew they could help us step more fully into our confidence? This book is for anyone ready to quiet the noise and claim their rightful place in any organization."

Liz Applegate, Business Mindset Coach

"Twenty succinct tips that are sure to make a difference in every introvert's life. Read it cover-to-cover or just start with the ones that jump out first. Get ready. Hall's wisdom and engagement is about to change your life."

Steve Friedman, award-winning author of **The Corporate Introvert: How to Lead and Thrive with Confidence** and creator of resources for introverts at BeyondIntroversion.com

STEP UP AND STAND OUT

20 TIPS FOR ASPIRING INTROVERTED LEADERS

Heather L Hall

Heather L Hall / Discover With Heather
Easton, MD

Step Up and Stand Out: 20 Tips for Aspiring Introverted Leaders / Heather L Hall. —1st ed.
Print ISBN 978-0-578-35264-0
Ebook ISBN 978-0-578-35265-7

Contents

Contents

Dedication

*For all the aspiring leaders
who feel unseen and unheard –
May you own your strengths,
trust your story, and
live success on your own terms.*

Introduction

Being an introvert doesn't mean you're shy, reticent, or reclusive; descriptions used by most dictionaries. Introverts are people who prefer calm, quiet environments. They prefer deep 1:1 conversations, rather than gathering in groups, and they usually enjoy alone time to recharge after social engagements. Introverts are perfectly normal and account for 30-50% of the population.

I've always enjoyed my alone time and found large gatherings to be exhausting. I rarely spoke first in meetings or rushed to make decisions, preferring to observe and do my research. So, early in my career, I wasn't surprised to learn that I was an introvert. In fact, knowing this is just how I'm wired gave me permission to be who I am and honor the gifts I bring to the team.

It wasn't until I entered the corporate environment that I realized being an introvert could have a negative impact on my career. It turns out that the business world (in the US, at least) was built *by* extroverts *for* extroverts. And their standard for leadership is bold, energetic, and outgoing.

Studies show that the majority of corporate executives in the US think introverts don't make good leaders. They consider us to be aloof, withdrawn, unfriendly and unsociable. Our quiet, observant, introspective behavior is seen as a detriment to success.

Where executives see what's missing, I see the secret superpowers of introverts.

We are strategic thinkers and solution-oriented problem-solvers due to our capacity for research and in-depth contemplation. The depth of our listening leads others to consider us close friends and confidants, building strong relationships and loyal followers. We tend to be avid readers and strong writers, facilitating clear communication. And our integrity and expertise can be intimidating to others.

These are just a few of the strengths which introverts bring to their teams. They are also the core skills which executives seek in leaders. So why aren't we sought out and promoted?

If you're like most of the introverts I work with, you've got skills, talent, and experience, but you don't go around bragging. You consistently contribute to the organization, but you're not getting recognized or rewarded like your colleagues. You may be the quietest person on the team, but that doesn't mean you're not engaged or working hard. You do your homework, bringing great ideas to meetings, but your boss often doesn't see or hear you. You have ambition, but your career has been stalled. And, when you are promoted, you find it exhausting, trying to fit in with the new team and expectations.

During my corporate career, I frequently bumped into assumptions and expectations about quiet leaders. I found ways around and through these barriers, while staying true to myself and achieving success on my own terms. I'm here to tell you that introverts *can* be successful leaders without conforming to the extroverted model. In fact, *introverts make great leaders!* Our ability to listen deeply, develop meaningful connections, research, and problem-solve in the toughest circumstances are just a few of the many characteristics of introverts which help us excel.

I wrote this book for the quiet leaders, struggling to rise up in their organizations. It is my hope that, by sharing my lessons learned, you can accelerate your own success.

If you're ready to **Step Up and Stand Out** – *without straying too far from your comfort zone* – this book is for you!

I encourage you to read the whole book, although you can do so in any order. You may want to try implementing a new tip each week or month, to give yourself ample opportunity to learn new skills. And spend some time with the *Questions for Reflection* at the end of each chapter. These will help you develop your personal action plan for success.

Tip #1: Embrace Your Superpowers

As an introvert, you're wired differently than most of your colleagues. But you have secret superpowers they can't touch.

You're more comfortable talking one-on-one and prefer meaningful conversations, while they're energized in group settings and easily chit-chat with everyone.

Introverts are super observant, natural born sociologists. While extroverts may think of you as a wallflower, that's just your way of stepping back to observe and catalog everything. You know what's going on around you and often have a sixth sense about people and situations.

You're a deep thinker, looking not just at what's happening in the moment, but processing what that means and what are the consequences. This makes you a great problem solver and – while you're reluctant to jump to conclusions – you are already identifying the gaps, collecting data, and running experiments in your mind.

Introverts are exceptional listeners. Many people think of us as great friends and confidants because we're so attentive. In a world that can't stop talking, as Susan Cain observes, being a listener is a rare and valued gift.

You bring a sense of calm to any room you enter. When you tap into it, your presence puts others at ease. You may lighten the tension or soothe the chaos in meetings. And, although you speak up less often, people listen when you do. Once people have a chance to know, like, and trust you, they will seek your input, recognizing that you've given the topic a great deal of thought.

Introverts tend to be avid readers with great recall and memory. They may not be the most spontaneous or articulate speakers, but they've done their research and are ready to expound upon their point of view when invited. In fact, if the topic is something they care deeply about, they're quite passionate and persuasive.

And you generally have strong communication skills, intentionally choosing your words to make your point and tuning into your audience to be sure you've been understood. Your team recognizes they can count on you to provide valuable insights, make connections which weren't obvious, and carry them forward with passion and dedication.

Don't internalize criticism from colleagues who cannot imagine how you manage to do what you do. Embrace your superpowers!

Questions for Reflection

- What are your introvert superpowers?

- How has each of them helped you to excel at what you do?

- Where (or when) do you find you need your superpowers the most?

Tip #2: Schedule "Me Time"

At home and at work, your ability to show up and deliver your best depends on your doing what you need to recharge your batteries.

As an introvert, you're better able to mingle with colleagues and clients when you've had some quiet time beforehand. You'll be able to recover from that big presentation if you give yourself some alone time after the event. And, if you've been pushing yourself for days or weeks on a big project, you'll need to schedule some down time to recuperate.

It took me years to learn the value of scheduling these "breaks," but the impact on my performance and attitude was remarkable. You may ask what took me so long to learn this lesson and I can only tell you it felt selfish to schedule "Me Time." It took a while for me to realize that I was able to be more present and productive, both at home and at work, when I built in the quiet time I needed to fill my cup.

Even the typical workday needs small buffers. Many of my introverted colleagues made a point to arrive a bit early so they could have a ½ hour to settle into the day before everyone arrived. As a night owl, I preferred the hour after everyone had left the office and the volume dropped 10 decibels, so I could finally hear myself think.

In most companies, scheduling meetings looks like an Olympic relay event. We run from one meeting to the next, often in the same conference room, without time to address action items or the opportunity to process what just happened. Now I use a scheduling app which lets me program breaks between meetings. This short buffer gives me a chance to catch my breath, reset my attention, and show up as my best self.

Questions for Reflection

- Which activities (e.g., meetings, presentations) would benefit from your taking some "Me Time"?

- What would "down time" look like after a big project? Would you need a day, a few days, or a week? Look at the next few months, pick a project and block out that time immediately afterwards.

- How often do you go from meeting to meeting without catching your breath? What if the default time (when a meeting is really needed, of course) was 45 minutes for the meeting followed by a 15 minute break?

Tip #3: Know Your "Why"

Many of the leaders I've met in my journey sought what others have – or what someone told them they're supposed to want – and they couldn't figure out why they felt dissatisfied in their careers and unhappy with their lives.

They may be striving for the fancy title, big raise, awards, or perks. Or they've already accumulated accolades and kept setting their sights on the "next big thing," rather than enjoying their success. In addition to the struggle and stress, they were always worried about tomorrow, unable to enjoy today.

When you set your goals based on what others want, your victories feel hollow. True satisfaction comes from within.

Spend time getting to know yourself. Find your "Why" – your higher purpose that inspires you. Align your actions with your reason for being here.

Purpose isn't something you pick at random. It's about honoring your unique gifts and applying them in a way that no one else can. It's your calling.

For most people, their purpose isn't the job itself. Some aspect of their work aligns with their purpose and brings them that feeling of being connected to something bigger than themselves. Others wander through jobs and relationships, unsure what they're looking for and unaware of their higher purpose. And some of us are lucky enough to earn our living through our vocation, being paid full-time for the work we were meant to do.

I've worked in teams where people with the same title and responsibilities got very different things out of the same work. One person thrived when troubleshooting, while another was happiest when they gathered and organized all the information, and the third relished reporting the results to the client. All of them could happily apply themselves to their purpose in other organizations or industries. Their sense of satisfaction came from aligning their efforts, and recognizing the outcome, when they applied themselves to their purpose.

Questions for Reflection

- What is your purpose? How does that show up in the work that you do (either paid or volunteer)?

- If you're not sure of your purpose, journal about the ways you contribute to your team, organization, community and family. Draw a line through the ones that drain your energy. Circle the ones which give you energy. Over the next few days, explore how your unique contributions giving meaning to your life.

Tip #4: Know and Honor Your Values

The dictionary tells us that "values" are those things with importance or significance to us. You may call them guiding principles or guideposts. I like to think of values as my internal compass, helping to guide me as I set goals and make decisions.

While our values may *seem* to be inherited, yours won't be exactly the same as your parent's. And, while you may have to *choose* one value over another, you don't pick your values, so it's unlikely yours are the same as your friend's or spouse's.

You see, they are unique to you, based on your lived experience. Your values are part of you, regardless of the situation. They are the basis for your decisions and, when you're aware of them, they can be quite helpful in making decisions.

The problem is, we sometimes find ourselves drifting out of alignment. When we find ourselves sacrificing our principles, regretting an upcoming commitment, suffering from burnout, we're either unclear of – or out of alignment with – our values.

Many of the clients I work with find a gap between the values they aspire to have and the values they actually practice. For example, you might aspire to be honest and live with integrity, but find yourself making excuses and letting things slide. Maybe you believe spending time with family is your #1 value, but find you're always working evenings and weekends or traveling for your job. Perhaps you're a leader who values people and relationships, but your job is totally focused on profits and metrics.

Sometimes we have to compromise on our values, justifying hard choices. When that becomes the norm, rather than the exception, these discrepancies – even the small ones – create stress and tension which lead to burnout.

Living out of alignment with our values happens because we aren't clear on our values and don't prioritize our resources accordingly, especially our time and money. Take the time to clarify your values and make sure you know your most important principles or guideposts when making decisions.

Questions for Reflection

- When are you most alive or engaged? What values are central to this experience?

- When are you most frustrated or angry? What values are being suppressed?

- When you have to make a major life decision, what are the "driving forces"?

- Who demonstrates values, principles, or guideposts that inspires you?

- What does it look like when you live according to your values?

Tip #5: Never Let Salary Define Your Worth

There's a lot of talk about our "value" and "worth," but most of it completely misses the mark. You cannot put a price on your value as an employee, a leader, or a human being.

You are priceless!

In our society, we are hired for a wage or salary which is set by the employer based on a number of variables. Some of the more obvious ones are industry, location, skill, education, certification, and experience. Less obvious, but of significant concern to the employer, is the benefits package. For most companies, this costs the employer an additional 30-40%.

As you consider a job offer or promotion, gather information on as many of these variables as possible and be sure you're not comparing apples to oranges. For example, I once worked with someone who couldn't secure the raise he wanted. With a growing family, he looked elsewhere and took the first job that offered him the salary he wanted. Unfortunately, he didn't realize that company only covered 50% of the employee's health insurance premiums, while our employer paid for 80% of this benefit, so his take home pay was lower. While he'd won a victory, he ended up falling short of his goal.

Keep in mind, your experience is priceless, too. I've known people who took lateral transfers every couple of years, just to gain experience in different roles and to build their network. In a relatively short time, they were well positioned to create their dream job and secure significantly higher salaries.

And, before any negotiation, know these two things:

1st = *The salary defines the job – not you!* Remember that you are worth more than you'll be paid.

2nd = *Everything is negotiable.* If you cannot get the promotion or the raise you seek, consider asking for something that's meaningful to you which is also in your boss's power to grant you. For example:

- better workspace because you'll be more productive away from all the distractions

- flexible schedule so you'll be more focused when you are at work

- reimbursement for a course or program you want to take which will help you develop a skillset or your knowledge base

- the opportunity to lead a particular project to demonstrate your abilities

- membership in a professional organization, or registration for a professional conference, where you can network while promoting your organization

- redistributing your workload for balance, efficiency, and/or diversity

- the opportunity to earn a bonus for meeting a specific goal

Questions for Reflection

- What are your "Non-negotiables" (both the "must-haves" and the "hard-noes")?

- What are your Desirables (which you'd like to have, but can live without)?

- What are your Undesirables (which you don't want, but can live with)?

Tip #6: Take a Seat at the Table

As introverts, we're more comfortable in the back seat, quietly observing. We're not likely to contribute to the discussion or volunteer for those tough assignments. Needless to say, we're less likely to be seen or heard.

To be recognized, we need to move up to the front row, speak up, and raise our hand to volunteer.

When I was first advised to take a seat at the table, I thought, "Those chairs are reserved for the people making a difference." Then I realized, I wanted to make a difference, too!

As my coach explained to me, if that seat was meant for someone else, I would be invited to move. In the meantime, the simple act of taking a seat at the table sent a clear signal to my manager that I was ready, willing, and able to contribute. As a result, they were more likely to remember and call upon me. And, once I had a proven track record of contributions, they started asking for my input.

Although it wasn't obvious in the beginning, I quickly came to realize that taking a seat at the table empowered me to show up, prepared and ready to contribute. By taking an "inner circle" chair, I was telling *myself* that my experience and contributions mattered. At the very least, I was challenging myself to "step it up a notch" and this helped me to lean into leadership.

I have attended lots of meetings where colleagues would rush to the outer circle of chairs. Perhaps they didn't know what message they were sending. Or they just didn't want to contribute. Maybe they didn't notice that sitting in the "cheap seats" didn't spare them the work! They were still assigned the bulk of the action items, but they didn't weigh in on the discussion and often left with frustration about their assignments. By taking a seat at the table, I was able to contribute to the discussion and help shape the outcome.

When you're first trying to demonstrate your leadership, much of what you do is behind the scenes and unrecognized. "Take a seat at the table" gave me permission to make my intentions obvious and it challenged me to up my game. As a result, I was able to shape decisions and receive recognition for my ideas.

Questions for Reflection

- When is the next time you will have an opportunity to take a seat at the table?

- How will you prepare for that meeting? What's one thing you can contribute? Note: If there isn't an agenda, stop by the organizers office and ask what to anticipate. Let them know you'd just like to come prepared to contribute.

- What do you want to get out of that meeting? Note: Start small. If you don't usually speak up, your first goal might be acknowledging someone else's contribution.

Tip #7: Lead from Your Heart

Many of the introverts I've known didn't think they were qualified for leadership roles. Most were discouraged by bosses who didn't appreciate their contributions. Others weren't willing to become who they thought they had to be to fit the expectations.

That's unfortunate because if there's one thing our corporate cultures need, it's introverted leaders!

They bring superpowers that their extroverted colleagues cannot access. (Refer to Tip #1) Introverts lead with intention and dedication, to the mission and their team. They have compassion and empathy for themselves and others. They strive for excellence and are willing to admit their mistakes. They speak truth and create safety for others to speak candidly. And introverts are lifelong learners who nurture and mentor others.

Introverted leaders are the more likely to be...
>...collaborative rather than autocratic
>...relational rather than transactional
>...motivated to be productive rather than by personal ambition and

> ...insightful, long-range planners and
> problem solvers, rather than quick fixers

If you're like me, you recognize that serving others is a key part of leadership. I take pride in that role and consider myself a Servant Leader. Unfortunately, most corporate executives don't understand the term "Servant Leader" (any more than they understand introverts), so you might be more comfortable identifying as a Values-Based Leader or Heart-Centered Leader.

You may still be learning about your leadership style. In that case, know that there are many types of leaders, and you don't have to do it quite like anyone else. So, if you've struggled to fit into the leadership mold according to someone else's terms, remember to know and honor your values. (Refer to Tip# 4) When you lead from your heart – with your values – then your authenticity will inspire trust and loyalty in others.

I recall a colleague who desperately wanted recognition and rewards, so much that his frustration would erupt from time to time, undermining his efforts. Once he recognized that he was bending over backwards to fit into someone's expectations – which didn't align with his values and gifts – he was able to stop acting out and start showing up as himself. When he tuned into his values, and began leading from his heart, new paths opened up and he became the leader of a new organization.

Questions for Reflection

- Who inspires you as a leader? (Select 2-3 people you know.)

- What about them inspires you?

- How do you want to show up as a leader?

Tip #8: Speak Early and Often

It's hard to be seen and heard when we don't speak up during meetings. It's even harder to speak up when we don't practice using our voice.

If you're going to capture your boss's attention – and give them reason to believe you can be an inspiring leader – you're going to have to speak up and speak persuasively.

At one time or another, we're all hesitant to speak publicly. In fact, fear of public speaking ranks as the leading fear for people worldwide. Even the phrase "public speaking" will cause the most competent and confident people to skip a heartbeat.

There are many things you can do to overcome this fear. I would say that practicing early and often is the best way to gain confidence, especially if you managed to arrive at this point in your career without experience standing in front of an audience.

If you're anything like me, you may have squeaked through school and college without ever giving a presentation. It just wasn't a requirement and who volunteers for such torture?!?

Then, without warning or preparation, I found myself in a graduate seminar class. Little did I know that "seminar" meant the students do the research, compose a report, and present it to the rest of the class and all the faculty of our department. Though I excelled at research and writing reports, the craft of composing or delivering a speech was a complete mystery. So, I read and reread it to myself until I had it almost memorized.

Let me assure you, what sounds good in your head doesn't always work well when you try to utter the words aloud, especially if your writing style favors those long sentences with several dependent clauses. Add to that, the anxiety of speaking and being judged, my heart was racing like a freight train and my mouth was going almost as fast! I finished my 45 minute presentation in less than 20 minutes!

My first career, as a college professor, gave me ample opportunity to improve my presentation skills. Even so, being the teacher gives you a false sense of comfort, as you are in control of the class.

Moving into the business world brought new challenges and many opportunities to practice the craft of persuasive speaking. Even as a seasoned speaker, I find each new audience elicits doubts and nervousness. I've learned to embrace my inner critic and recognize the sensation as a sign that this work matters to me. Confidence comes, after the presentation, as the audience engages with me and my message.

Questions for Reflection

- Where (or with whom) can you practice speaking in a safe setting?

- What's something you're passionate about? Practice speaking about that topic with a friend.

Tip #9: Invest in Pockets

Being service-oriented can be a blessing and a curse. On the one hand, you get to learn more than you would if you stayed in your lane and did only your work. However, if you're anything like me, you'll also spend so much time helping others, you end up working late to complete your own projects. Eventually you might wonder if you're a human magnet for other people's problems.

My love of puzzles and research prompted me to roll up my sleeves and take on many problems that wouldn't have crossed my desk otherwise. I enjoyed the challenge and felt a sense of pride, being able to resolve the tough ones.

Then it was pointed out that some people were dropping their problems on me because they knew I couldn't say "No"! As you can imagine, it hurt to be taken advantage of and was embarrassing to be manipulated.

As a problem-solver, I got curious and soon found a way to demagnetize: Pants with Pockets! Now, instead of instinctively reaching out for the file they were handing me, I would put my hands in my pockets and say, "Tell me more." This gave me a few minutes to consider whether theirs was a problem that I should take on or (more likely) if this was a teaching moment where I might help them build their skillset.

This was a tough lesson in the importance of healthy boundaries and a pivot point in my journey towards leadership.

Most of us are afraid to set boundaries, in both our professional and personal lives. We worry about hurting someone's feelings, making them angry, or not being liked. However, in reality, the lack of boundaries is a problem for both parties.

Though it will take some practice, it is possible to set and maintain boundaries which help you to be more productive, happier, and a better leader. Get curious about where your time and energy are being drained. (This may be the person who stops by to chat for 30 minutes or the colleague who waits until the last minute to start their part of your team project.) Clarify your priorities and where others are interfering with your productivity. State your boundary, clearly and respectfully. Be prepared to repeat this several times, especially if you've been enabling others for a while.

Questions for Reflection

- In what ways do others drain your time and energy?

- What could you say to let them know you have a boundary?

- Who can you practice with, so you get comfortable stating your boundary?

- How will your life be better when they're not draining your time and energy?

Tip #10: Stop and Smell the Roses

If there's one thing I've learned over the years, it's the importance of pausing and being present.

In my struggle to gain approval and recognition, I spent too much time trying to do #*AllTheThings*. When I was in my head, my thoughts would flip between obsessing about what I'd said at that meeting earlier and worrying about that project I needed to complete by tomorrow. There wasn't time to relax or catch my breath. And I wasn't good at shutting down work at the end of the day and getting on with my life.

Although most introverts are not workaholics, most workaholics are introverts. There's a fine line between diligence and perfectionism. And it's too easy to slide from dutiful to overcommitted.

I was pre-disposed to be a workaholic. When I couldn't manage issues in my personal life, I'd consoled myself by diving into the work. After all, work was the one place I knew I could excel. When I finally tried to live a more well-rounded life, I ended up adding more and more obligations on top of an overloaded schedule, rather than balancing my priorities with my time and energy.

Friends and family had counseled me to slow down and pace myself. My boss even suggested I lighten up, but neither of us could figure out who would take care of #AllTheThings.

For me, burning the candle at both ends had become a way of life. So, perhaps I shouldn't have been surprised to wake up on a two-lane highway, going 60 mph, in the wrong lane. I swerved right to avoid a head-on collision, then swerved left to avoid going over the embankment. Narrowly passing between two oncoming cars, I rolled down the opposite embankment, landing in the marsh.

Thankfully, no one was hurt, except my pride and my brand-new SUV. While my vehicle was in the shop, I searched for a therapist to address my underlying issues. From there, I began my search for happiness, balance, and the ability to stop and smell the roses.

After years of trying to be what I thought was required to prove myself, I finally learned to align with my core values and focus on my priorities. It took a few years, but I'm healthier and happier than I've ever been, and you can be, too.

Questions for Reflection

- What are your core values? Are your choices aligned?

- Do you spend more time "Being" or "Doing"?

- What would it be like for you to stop and smell the roses? How can you build this into your daily routine?

Tip #11: Empowerment is an Inside Job

While it's important to have a boss who empowers their employees, it's vital to have employees who are self-empowered. Organizations cannot make progress if their staff are dependent on their managers for every decision.

Your growth as an individual – and especially as a leader – will be limited by the degree to which you're waiting for someone else to give you permission to make decisions and take action. Your ability to act with autonomy, determining and taking the next right step, is key for your success.

When managers look for emerging leaders, they're seeking the people in their organization who are the "Go Getters" and "Doers;" those who are self-empowered.

You are that person!

As an introvert, you are already observing and analyzing what works and what doesn't. You have a vision of what needs to be done and a strategy to accomplish that. When you take initiative and follow through, you are demonstrating leadership.

Each time you identify and implement a solution, based on your experience and instincts, you're demonstrating your agency. When you find yourself at a crossroads, assess the options, and take the next step, you are exercising your empowerment.

This doesn't mean you have to do everything yourself. In some cases, you'll roll up your sleeves and do the thing. At other times, you'll delegate. More often, you will collaborate and coordinate with others.

One of my clients was in a new role for a different division of their organization. Although her duties were essentially the same, there were new stakeholders, projects, and colleagues. In her old role, the projects were shared by an assigned team; however, the new role required her to enlist collaborators. Her success depended on her ability to build and lead the team, which required her initiative and self-empowerment.

Questions for Reflection

- Where are you most comfortable making decisions and taking action?

- What more could you accomplish if you trusted your own instincts?

- Find an opportunity to live into your empowerment this week.
  How did it feel? If you found yourself apologizing for doing the right thing, find another opportunity and celebrate your success unapologetically.

Tip #12: Be Solution-Oriented

It's in your nature to spot the problems. As an introvert, you have a discerning eye, so you easily recognize what's missing or out of alignment. And, because you're always assessing, you have keen insights about that situation.

What you do with that information will make all the difference in your leadership journey.

If you stay in your comfort zone and keep your thoughts to yourself, you're not serving the team, clients, or yourself. With time, your awareness will lead to frustration and disgruntlement. Before you know it, you're complaining out loud about the way things have always been, without recognizing you contributed to that problem.

If you do speak up, but bring only criticism, you're disruptive and destructive. It won't take many encounters before you're labeled as negative and hard to work with.

The way to use your secret superpowers (Refer to Tip #1) for the greater good is to identify the problem AND offer potential solutions.

You're not responsible for always bringing the best solution. It's not about being the hero or being right all the time. It's about building upon what you have, instead of destroying it. It's about seeing and acting upon opportunities for improvement.

I was fortunate that I'd learned this lesson before the company where I worked adopted Lean, a continuous improvement program. Because I'd built trust and respect, I was able to channel my discernment for problems into finding solutions which helped our organization.

But I had to start small and build my reputation as a team player. I had to demonstrate that I was concerned with the greater good, not just what's in it for me. It wasn't long before I was collaborating and coordinating with others, testing ideas to make their jobs easier and more productive. In time, I was championing projects across departments and contributing to the bottom line.

Use your curiosity and powers of research for the greater good. You'll make your job easier and you'll be well on your way to a promotion.

Questions for Reflection

- What's one problem that affects your work and you see a solution?

- Who else is impacted by this problem?

- Whose buy-in do you need to move forward with your solution?

- How did it feel to implement this improvement?

- What's the next problem you will address?

Tip #13: Be a Team Player

If you're anything like me, you grew up preferring solo activities. Group activities, team sports, and team projects were dreaded.

While I started my career in solo roles, I noticed that the world works in teams and realized that I would forever limit my opportunities if I didn't learn how to join them. So, when I interviewed for my first corporate role and was asked the familiar question about strengths and weaknesses, I shared that my strength was my independence *and* – even though I didn't have much experience working in team settings – it was my goal to be an effective team member and I was looking forward to the opportunity.

You can probably guess the weakness in my plan: Setting a goal, without clear objectives, didn't make it come true. It took me a while to understand how I fit into the team and a bit longer to learn how to build successful teams.

By applying my introvert superpowers (Refer to Tip #1), I learned the "4C"s of great teamwork:

Connection: Introverts excel at creating relationships. We may not want to chit-chat at the watercooler, but we're all in for a deep conversation about our work, hobbies, or passion projects. And – what amazes colleagues or clients who don't get to see us often – we remember what others have shared with us.

Coordination: With our "Spidey senses," introverts naturally know how to juggle all the tasks and timelines so that projects are managed efficiently.

Collaboration: When we're in touch with our intuition, we're able to assess what members of the team need to be more effective. We instinctively develop systems which support our team.

Communication: If you think of a leader you've known who was a great communicator – though not necessarily a motivational or charismatic speaker – chances are that person was an introvert. They understood that communication is a two-way process and practiced active listening, asking questions, and making space for your answers. They were skilled at non-verbal communication and recognized that less is more, so they were succinct. And they follow up, asking questions which let you know they remember what matters to you or circling back to be sure their message was received.

When you practice these skills, you develop trust and loyalty.

Bonus Tip: Make time to socialize with colleagues outside of the office. You can find calm venues – like a quiet café, a relaxed lunch spot, or a coffee chat via Zoom – for one-on-one or small group meetings which won't exhaust you. I found myself in a bowling league with colleagues where we discovered we enjoyed each other's company – without the stress of the job. We developed friendships which helped up to more productive at work.

Questions for Reflection

- Get curious about yourself at work this week. Where are you engaging with your team? Where you're avoiding others, maintaining your independence?

- What might be possible if you were to practice the "4C"s of great teamwork?

Tip #14: Let Go to Move Forward

We all want to do a good job and it can take a while, after starting a new job or taking on new responsibilities, to feel competent and comfortable in our role. After a while, we may cling to that comfort and avoid leaning into our growth edge.

Over the years, I've seen many introverts – myself included – cling to tasks and jobs which are familiar, thereby limiting their capacity.

These are not necessarily easy tasks. In fact, they're often complicated procedures which we know no one else wants to do.

Maybe it's a sense of pride, that we're able to do the challenging thing. Or the feeling of control, that we'd just have to fix it anyway, so we might as well do it ourselves.

But here's the thing: If you cannot let go of those tasks, you will not have the time or energy to take on new responsibilities and you will remain stuck in your current role. The harder you work to prove you are important because you can do the thing no one else can, the more you will undermine your efforts to succeed.

In all fairness, many people are happy with their job, just as it is. I'm going to guess, however, that you aren't reading this book because you want to stay where you are.

If you are ready for opportunities, you will need to try new things and take on additional responsibilities. That might involve some risk, but it will be even harder if you are burdened with all the old duties. Besides, in most organizations, you will need to train others to take on your current duties so that you can be promoted. And, from a sustainability perspective, there should always be more than one person capable of performing key functions.

This will feel scary, letting go of your sense of security or identity. It can also feel liberating.

At one point in my career, I was selected for a transfer overseas. I had trained my successor and colleagues, but the transfer was delayed. For the next few months, I literally lived in the wake of my succession. I felt untethered, as I waited on standby, and unsure of my future. This time also gave me an opportunity to recognize my best contributions to the home team and to create a new role for myself.

Questions for Reflection

- Which of your tasks have no backup?
  Who would be a good person to train so
  that you can take vacation time without
  being called to help?

- What's a task that a colleague performs
  without backup which you would like to
  learn?

- Imagine the monkey bars on an
  elementary school playground and each
  bar represents your progress through the
  corporate ladder. What do you need to
  release to grab ahold of the next bar?

Tip #15: Own Your Story

As an introvert, you tend to sit back, listening and observing, instead of leaning into the conversation. In a group of strangers, even colleagues you've met a few times, you're likely to go radio silent. However, in a group of friends or trusted colleagues, you're chatting and contributing from the beginning.

If you've worked with the same team for a while, and you trust them enough to speak up, they might be surprised to learn you're an introvert. That was my experience.

During a teambuilding exercise, we had to go around the table, each sharing a story about ourselves that the others didn't know. When it came to my turn, I hesitated and took a minute to gather my thoughts before sharing. One of my friends, noticing my discomfort, asked why that was so hard for me. When I responded, "Because I'm an introvert," half the group – the extroverted half – was shocked. They'd known me for years and didn't believe that was true.

How did I manage to rise to the occasion? Trust. I knew these people well, trusted myself to select an appropriate story, and trusted them with what I shared.

If you're anything like me, you already know that I spoke haltingly, unsure of myself, and disbelieving anyone would want to hear about me. Introverts don't talk much about ourselves and tend to be extremely private. We have a difficult time articulating our feelings or emotions and are hesitant to share our thoughts and opinions, especially in groups.

Is it any wonder that quiet leaders struggle in social gatherings where we're meeting clients or new colleagues? Parties where you're expected to mingle are the extroverts happy place, but they're torture for introverts.

My best tip for surviving social settings is two-fold:

1. Prepare several questions to ask. Select topics which are general, like favorite hobbies/activities or recent vacations.

2. Plan to share a couple stories which aren't too personal. Safe topics might include: a book you recently read, a popular movie or TV show you've just watched, a favorite museum or popular event.

And in the office, where you have built trust with your boss and colleagues, own your introversion. Avoid labels or limitations, but don't be afraid to share your superpowers. (Refer to Tip #1) A healthy appreciation of your contributions and needs will make it easier for them to honor your boundaries. (Refer to Tip #8)

One warning: Don't use your introversion as an excuse. The goal is to stretch ourselves; not to make excuses for staying stuck.

Questions for Reflection

- What would it be like to be accepted as an introvert?

- What's one questions you wish people would ask you?

- What's one personal story you would like to share with others?

Tip #16: Take Up Space

Although we want to be seen and heard, introverts apply a lot of energy to hiding. In addition to becoming a wallflower in social situations, we go out of our way to be sure we don't draw attention to ourselves. We avoid taking up space – in the office, at meetings, on our boss's calendar – or other people's time.

Here's the thing: As aspiring leaders, we need to step up and stand out.

Managers cannot recognize and reward you if you don't contribute. While there are opportunities to contribute 1:1 outside of the boardroom, it is vital that you demonstrate your expertise in meetings with your colleagues and managers.

In addition to taking a seat at the table (Refer to Tip #6), get on the meeting agenda and get in front of the room to address topics of concern, especially when your boss or your boss's boss is attending. Volunteer for new assignments, making a point to be seen contributing. And take the lead on passion projects where you can demonstrate your commitment to the mission and success.

With a little planning and practice, you can make a positive impact and a favorable impression. I've worked with several colleagues who joined Toastmasters to gain confidence with public speaking. They became persuasive speakers and successful leaders. By showing up, and being seen as a contributor, you will be remembered as a valuable member of the team.

I can hear you, thinking you don't have anything to say, but I don't believe that. As an introvert, you're always gathering and synthesizing information. You know the strengths, weaknesses, opportunities and threats for your organization. Your insights and suggestions can make a big difference for your clients and colleagues. Even small contributions add up over time and lead to the recognition and rewards you seek.

Questions for Reflection

- Where are you hiding?

- How can you step up and stand out more?

- What's one thing you wish your team was paying more attention to?

- When and where is the best place to share your suggestions with them?

Tip #17: Toot Your Own Horn

Even if you've embraced every tip so far, you probably got to this one and said, "Umm...No!"

I get it. Tooting your own horn is harder than taking a seat at the table, speaking up, standing out, and taking up space – combined! The idea of talking about our accomplishments feels exhausting and reeks of bragging to an introvert.

What if I told you that highlighting your contributions for your boss is actually doing them a service?

Even when your accomplishments are visible, expecting your boss to remember is asking a lot. They have their own challenges, and your contributions may not be top of mind when it matters, like during your annual review.

Much of the great work you do is behind the scenes, so your boss won't know if you don't bring it to their attention. Make a point to have regular check-in meetings and bring them up to speed. Focus on impacts and outcomes, rather than the individual tasks.

Don't be shy about asking clients or colleagues, who offer you praise, to share their feedback with your boss. A short message of appreciation will make a big impression.

And those brilliant ideas you shared in a meeting, that weren't acknowledged until someone else shared them? Take them back! Don't give into your frustration by claiming credit for the idea. Leverage the moment by sharing your expertise, mentioning what inspired you (e.g., a client suggesting or article you read), sharing the data you discovered in your research, and explaining how you envision implementing the plan.

Questions for Reflection

- Start keeping a file of your accomplishments. Be sure to include praise you've received from clients and colleagues.

- When was the last time you shared an accomplishment with your boss? Make a point of sharing this week. Remember to focus on the outcomes, not tasks.

- If you have a regular weekly or biweekly check-in with your boss, make a point to share a win at each meeting. If you have to share a failure, bring two wins.

- If you don't have a regularly scheduled meeting, can you schedule one or establish a routine of informal chats?

- And, if your only facetime with your boss is at the weekly team meeting, suggest adding "celebrations" to the agenda. We could all use more celebrations!

Tip #18: Don't Give Away Your Power

It took me a long time to understand why my leadership coach kept asking, "Why give away your power?" When we first started working together, early in my leadership journey, I didn't realize what I was doing. It took a while for me to recognize when I was giving away my power and even longer to realize it was a choice I was making.

Many of the clients I work with share the same struggle.

The most common patterns I see are:

1. We let others make decisions for us. Sometimes this happens because we delay or refuse to make a decision, thereby choosing the default option.

2. We let our emotions get in the way of responding professionally. When we react with anger or hurt feelings, we lose control of the situation.

3. We don't set or maintain healthy boundaries. (Refer to Tip #9)

In work, as in life, there is little that is in our control. How we show up is our biggest asset and will have the greatest impact on our professional and personal performance.

As introverts, we don't have the boundless energy which extroverts seem to possess. We cannot afford to give away our power by fretting over choices we are well equipped to make or regretting the outcomes, allowing our emotions to derail us, or being blindsided and railroaded by others.

Whether you know exactly what I mean and you're wondering how to break the habit, or you believe these scenarios are not an issue for you, try this exercise for the next month: Make a daily practice of reviewing your day and identifying at least one thing that lifted you up or filled your cup, as well as one thing that drained you. After a few weeks, review your notes for trends and identify which of the above situations seems to be the biggest culprit. Awareness of the problem is half of the solution.

Questions for Reflection

- How do you give away your power?

- What is the impact when you give away your power?

- What more could you achieve if you didn't give away your power?

- What are some immediate steps you can take to reclaim your power?

Tip #19: Your Voice is Powerful

Unlike your extroverted colleagues, who never lack for something to say, your voice speaks volumes.

Among colleagues and clients who have gotten to know you, they recognize you don't speak up unless you have something worth sharing. They respect the depth of your experience and veracity of your research. So, when you speak up, you have their full attention.

Your inner critic – that inner voice which tells you, "No one cares what you have to say!" or "Wait until you have all the facts!" – is wrong! Thank them for trying to protect you, then remind them *you've got this.* You've done your homework. You're ready to deliver. And it's time for your inner critic to trust you.

If there's one tip I would give managers to help them nurture the introverts on their team, it is to make space for everyone to contribute. If they can honor the fact that introverts need a little more time to process what they're thinking, and to invite "those we haven't heard from" to share their thoughts, everyone would benefit from their experience and insights.

When you own your superpowers and your story
(Refer to Tips #1 and #15), you can help your
boss develop a stronger team by embracing the
other half of their staff. And, as you lead
meetings, you can model this by facilitating the
conversation so that everyone is encouraged and
expected to contribute.

Questions for Reflection

- Do you have an introverted colleague
  who is comfortable speaking up? Observe
  them to see what makes them effective.
  Ask them for pointers. If you're in the
  same meetings, ask for support so that
  you can share your voice, too.

- When have you felt comfortable speaking
  up during meetings? What made this
  possible?

- What would be possible if you spoke up
  more often?

Tip #20: Create Your Own Board of Directors

In my leadership journey, I recognized that I couldn't do it alone. I needed to understand expectations which weren't written in our employee manual. I wanted to try out ideas that weren't documented in our standard operating procedures. And I needed perspectives that were beyond my experience.

I found myself seeking answers from a variety of people who I came to consider as my personal "Board of Directors." Each of these trusted advisors supported and encouraged me. Although we never gathered all together, I consulted with each of them on a regular basis. These mentors shared their insights and recommendations without attachment. They modeled inspiring leadership for me. To have their support and encouragement helped me to become more than I was and more than I knew I could be.

Your personal Board of Directors is not a formal group, like the BoD for a company or nonprofit organization. They don't actually get a vote on what you do or how you do it! They might not even realize they hold a special role in your life.

Although I do hope you will express your appreciation for them!

They are advisors and mentors who know you by name and want what is best for you. They know about your hopes and dreams. They see your gifts and encourage you to develop them. They are people you connect with in real life – by phone, email, snail mail or in person – and, when you do connect, you feel their support and guidance.

They don't have to be inside your organization. They don't have to be in a position to get you that dream job. They don't have to be anything like you. In fact, the more variety in their viewpoints, the better!

Reach out, just to let them know you're thinking of them and ask for an opportunity to connect with them. Without asking for anything in return, let them know what you're up to these days. Take the opportunity to let them know the impact they've had on your personal and/or professional development.

Keep in mind that these connections don't need to be frequent. For most of them, you might only connect once a year. And understand that you will probably be the one reaching out. If you're not comfortable networking, it may take a little practice.

You may tell me that you hate networking and I'm right there with you. However, as an introvert, you do nurture deep relationships and that's what we're talking about with your BoD. They don't need to know everything about you, but you have the opportunity to share more than just the surface with them.

I've known most of my mentors for a decade or more, one of them since I was 16 years old, while others were in my life for just a season. Some of these folks I saw or spoke with regularly, but most were rare conversations, emails or letters. What they all have in common is that they answered when I reached out. They could set aside their own self-interest to consider what I was saying and needing. They shared their wisdom and gave sound advice.

Questions for Reflection

- Who are you already connected to that fits this role of informal mentor or advisor? How can you nurture your relationship?

- Who have you met that you would like to connect with?

- Who would you like to meet, to develop a relationship, and who can introduce you?

- Who can you support as a mentor or advisor? Imagine what it would feel like if someone you influenced reached out to you. Be that person.

Conclusion

When you **Step Up and Stand Out** – *without straying too far from your comfort zone* – you can achieve the recognition and rewards you deserve.

Remember to get clear on your superpowers and honor your values. Practice taking a seat at the table, raising your hand, and speaking up. (I promise, it will become easier with practice.) Be sure to build in plenty of "me time" and maintain healthy boundaries.

Review your answers to the *Questions for Reflection* at the end of each chapter. Which action plans have you already implemented? Which will give you the biggest return on investment? Where can you get support and encouragement during your leadership journey?

Feel free to reach out to me with any questions and to share your wins. I'd love to support you and cheer you on! You'll find me on LinkedIn, Instagram and Facebook.

Acknowledgements

To my #1 fan – Dad:
Thank you for always believing in me.
Your support means the world to me.

To the Managers and Colleagues
who learned and grew with me:
Thank you for your patience,
curiosity, and encouragement.

To my personal Board of Directors:
Thank you for always being there,
providing perspective, and
cheering me along the way.
I wouldn't be here without you.

www.ingramcontent.com/pod-product-compliance
Lightning Source LLC
Chambersburg PA
CBHW011846200326
41597CB00028B/4720